HOW TO GROW
GREENS

HOW TO GROW
GREENS

A GARDENER'S GUIDE TO GROWING CABBAGES, BRUSSELS SPROUTS, BROCCOLI, KALE, LETTUCE, CAULIFLOWER AND SPINACH, WITH STEP-BY-STEP TECHNIQUES AND OVER 150 PHOTOGRAPHS

RICHARD BIRD

southwater

This edition is published by Southwater, an imprint of Anness Publishing Ltd, Hermes House, 88–89 Blackfriars Road, London SE1 8HA; tel. 020 7401 2077; fax 020 7633 9499

www.southwaterbooks.com
www.annesspublishing.com

If you like the images in this book and would like to investigate using them for publishing, promotions or advertising, then please visit our website www.practicalpictures.com for more information.

UK distributor: Book Trade Services; tel. 0116 2759086; fax 0116 2759090; uksales@booktradeservices.com; exportsales@booktradeservices.com
North American distributor: National Book Network; tel. 301 459 3366; fax 301 429 5746; www.nbnbooks.com
Australian distributor: Pan Macmillan Australia; tel. 1300 135 113; fax 1300 135 103; customer.service@macmillan.com.au
New Zealand distributor: David Bateman Ltd; tel. (09) 415 7664; fax (09) 415 8892

Publisher: Joanna Lorenz
Managing Editor: Judith Simons
Project Editor: Felicity Forster
Editor: Lydia Darbyshire
Photographers: Jonathan Buckley, Amanda Heywood and Patrick McLeavey
Illustrator: Liz Pepperell
Designer: Louise Kirby
Editorial Reader: Penelope Goodare
Production Controller: Joanna King

ETHICAL TRADING POLICY
Because of our ongoing ecological investment programme, you, as our customer, can have the pleasure and reassurance of knowing that a tree is being cultivated on your behalf to naturally replace the materials used to make the book you are holding. For further information about this scheme, go to www.annesspublishing.com/trees

Previously published as *Growing Greens*

PUBLISHER'S NOTE
Although the advice and information in this book are believed to be accurate and true at the time of going to press, neither the authors nor the publisher can accept any legal responsibility or liability for any errors or omissions that may have been made nor for any inaccuracies nor for any loss, harm or injury that comes about from following instructions or advice in this book.

Contents

Introduction

Anyone who is interested in what they eat will do well to consider the practicalities of growing their own vegetables. Mounting concerns about the residues of fungicides, pesticides, artificial fertilizers and other chemicals in and on our foods have been intensified by the use of genetically modified crops and the dawning realization that it is almost impossible to know exactly what it is that we are putting in our mouths.

Growing vegetables in our own gardens, on even a small scale, can help to redress the balance. When you eat salad crops and winter greens that you have grown yourself from seed or from plantlets bought from a reputable supplier, you know that they are free from all taint of chemical. Even if you choose not to grow organically, you can use the minimum of artificial pesticides and fertilizers and time the applications so that you do not eat anything that has been recently sprayed.

GROWING FOR FLAVOUR

The pre-packaged produce we buy in supermarkets and large food stores may look appetizing and tempting, but how often the vegetables disappoint us when they are arranged on the serving dish. Tasteless, limp lettuces and bland, colourless cabbages are enough to put anyone off eating vegetables for life. Yet when these vegetables are fresh from the garden and cultivars have been selected for flavour instead of appearance and shelf-life, they bring interest, texture and taste to a range of dishes.

All greens are excellent sources of essential vitamins and minerals. Some, including salad leaves, spinach and cabbage, contain two powerful antioxidants, vitamin C and beta carotene, which boost and protect the immune system. Also, cruciferous vegetables, including broccoli, cabbages, cauliflowers,

BELOW The decorative quality of vegetables can be clearly seen in these rows. All the leaves are green and yet the variety of greens and the shapes of the leaves form a very attractive picture over a long season.

Brussels sprouts, kale and chard, are packed with phytochemicals, which numerous studies have shown can play a vital role in fighting disease.

GROWING FOR VARIETY

The bland uniformity of so much that is on offer in food stores is another reason more and more people recognize the benefits of devoting part of their garden to producing a few vegetables for the table. People with only small plots, who do not have space for a special vegetable garden, are finding that even in small corners it is possible to grow a surprising range of vegetables.

The old-fashioned cottage garden contained flowers and vegetables, growing together in carefree abandon. Gardeners can still achieve this type of exuberant planting by including leafy greens and even Brussels sprouts in beds and borders.

DECORATIVE GARDENING

Most people's idea of a vegetable garden is to have row upon row of worthy but essentially dull-looking green plants, surrounded by bare earth and giving the impression that looking after them is hard work. The reality need not be anything like this, and a glance through the catalogues of seed merchants and mail order suppliers will show a huge range of plants with every

RIGHT A harvest of fresh vegetables, including cauliflower, Savoy cabbage, Brussels sprouts, spinach, broccoli, kale and red-stemmed Swiss chard.

possible leaf colour and shape that can be grown as easily as favourite bedding plants.

Among the most decorative vegetables are the many types of salad crops, which are not only tasty and nutritious but also colourful. Choose from among the chards, with their vivid red stalks and red-veined green leaves. Red orach also has red stems, but the leaves are flushed and edged with red or with purple, depending on the cultivar. Mustard spinach has slightly glaucous leaves, while the finely divided kales and pretty mizunas and mibunas look almost too beautiful to eat.

ABOVE Calabrese broccoli, lightly steamed and served with fried garlic slices and a light soy sauce, is a wonderfully simple and healthy dish that cooks in minutes.

types of
greens

This group of vegetables covers a
wide range, from leafy salad crops to
creamy-white cauliflowers and purple
sprouting broccoli. What these vegetables
have in common is that they are all easily
within the capability of amateur gardeners
to grow and to grow well. Although the
first-time gardener will probably not
want to try more than two or three types,
more experienced gardeners will want
to include as many as possible. All
gardeners, however, will find that
growing these vegetables at home
provides tasty and nutritious greens for
the table almost all year round.

Cabbages

These have been in cultivation for 3,000 years or so, but the cabbage we know today is a comparatively recent development, probably dating from the Middle Ages. Cabbage can be found growing in the wild throughout Europe, but this form is more akin to broccoli than the hearted varieties with which we are familiar.

Cabbages come in various forms, mainly depending on the time of year they are harvested – spring, summer, autumn and winter varieties are self-evidently named. These are all hearting cabbages, although spring cabbage is also available as greens, which are loose heads of green leaves, unlike the typical tight heads of blanched leaves. A few other winter varieties are sometimes considered separately, including the Savoys (with their distinctive, crinkly leaves), and hybrids between the Savoys and winter cabbages. The most distinctive of the winter varieties is the red cabbage.

Some people have been put off cabbage by having to eat overcooked leaves, but it has always been a staple winter vegetable for gardeners and is delicious when properly cooked. It is a valuable source of vitamins C and E, potassium and beta carotene.

cabbage

red cabbage

Savoy cabbage

loose-leaf cabbage

green cabbage

winter cabbage

Brussels sprouts

The name of Brussels sprouts arose because they are thought to have originated in Belgium, where they are recorded as growing in the mid-18th century. By the beginning of the 19th century they had spread to France and Britain.

Even after 200 years of cultivation, Brussels sprouts still seem to be an acquired taste. Not everybody likes their distinctive, rather nutty flavour, and children in particular seem to find that they have too strong a taste. When they are cooked properly, however, they are a very tasty and valuable part of winter meals – they contain significant amounts of vitamin C and iron – and few people would consider their Christmas dinner complete without a bowl of them.

BELOW These Brussels sprouts are just beginning to develop. Soon the lower leaves will be removed, exposing the sprouts.

Brussels sprouts are usually categorized according to season: early, mid-season and late. If plants are grown from each group, there can be a continuous crop from autumn right through to spring.

The sprouts themselves, which resemble miniature cabbages, are the tight buds that form where the leaves join the main stem. As well as the sprouts, the succulent tops of the plants can be harvested once the sprouts are finished. The size of the plant varies according to cultivar, and some that have been bred as dwarf or compact plants are best suited to smaller gardens where space is at a premium. The early-cropping 'Peer Gynt', for example, is a dwarf, compact form. Another intriguing type is the red-leaved variety 'Rubine', which is ideal for decorative kitchen gardens. A new variety, 'Falstaff', has purple sprouts that retain their colour when cooked.

VARIETIES

Early
'Lancelot'
'Oliver'
'Peer Gynt'

Mid-season
'Bedford Fillbasket'
'Citadel'
'Evesham Special'
'Mallard'
'Roger'

Late
'Fortress'
'Icarus'
'Sheriff'
'Trafalgar'
'Widgeon'

COOKING SPROUTS

Trim away the bottom of the stalk and outer leaves. Cut large sprouts in half. Cook for 3–5 minutes in boiling salted water until just tender.

Brussels sprouts

Sprouting broccoli

Broccoli was developed from the wild cabbage in the 17th century in Italy, from where it spread through the rest of Europe. Calabrese broccoli (or Italian sprouting broccoli) is the type normally sold in shops as broccoli. Romanesco (Roman broccoli) is another similar plant, but in the garden and kitchen they are considered separately from sprouting broccoli because they grow at a different time of year and are cultivated differently. Broccoli, particularly if eaten raw, contains plenty of B vitamins, vitamin C and iron.

It is the flower shoots of sprouting broccoli that are gathered and eaten, just as the buds are forming and before the yellow of the opening flowers is seen. The flowerheads appear both at the top of the plant and as side shoots. In most varieties the flower buds are purple – hence one of the alternative names, purple sprouting broccoli – but there are also creamy-white varieties, on which the

purple sprouting broccoli

VARIETIES

'Claret' (late)
'Early Purple Sprouting' (early to late)
'Nine Star Perennial' (mid-season)
'Purple Sprouting' (mid- to late)
'Rudolph' (early)
'White Sprouting' (mid- to late)
'White Star' (late)

flower buds appear like miniature cauliflowers. The purple varieties are generally considered to be hardier than the white forms.

There is one variety, 'Nine Star Perennial', which is, as its name suggests, perennial in habit. If all the heads are picked each year it should last up to about five years, producing white heads each year.

In addition to the flowerheads, the stalk just below the buds and their associated leaves can also be eaten. Even more stalk may be eaten if the tougher outside is first removed.

The harvesting period for sprouting broccoli varies slightly, but it fills the gap between late winter – 'Rudolph' is one of the earliest varieties – and mid-spring, when fresh vegetables are at a premium. The problem is that they are large plants and occupy the land for the best part of the year. Use the space between plants when they are first planted out for catch crops such as radishes. Each plant usually produces plenty of shoots and if space is limited, it is worth growing just a couple of plants.

LEFT Sprouting broccoli

Calabrese broccoli

Although calabrese broccoli (Italian sprouting broccoli) is in many ways very similar to sprouting broccoli, it is usually considered as a separate vegetable. Its origins are the same: it originated in the countries of the eastern Mediterranean and in Italy, before moving to the rest of Europe. It is sometimes known as Italian broccoli or American broccoli. Calabrese is healthy to eat, containing B vitamins, vitamin C and iron.

Unlike sprouting broccoli, calabrese is quick growing but not very hardy, and it is grown so that the edible heads, which are much larger than those of sprouting broccoli, are produced in late summer and autumn. It forms a large central head, which is rather like a loose cauliflower, and when this is picked, side shoots develop, each carrying a slightly smaller head. Not all varieties of calabrese broccoli seem capable of producing side shoots, however, and these varieties are finished once the main head has been picked.

Unlike sprouting broccoli, calabrese broccoli has a blue-green tinge. Another difference is that its growth should not be checked, so calabrese broccoli is sown where it is to grow and should not be transplanted.

Romanesco (Roman broccoli), sometimes also known as green cauliflower, is similar to calabrese broccoli and is, in fact, often listed as a variety of calabrese. The main difference is that it is hardier and can be grown to produce heads from late autumn into early winter, which means that it covers at least part of the gap between calabrese and sprouting broccoli.

Romanesco produces only a single head and is then finished. The shape of the head is also different from calabrese broccoli. It has a distinctly conical shape, with little eruptions over the surface, creating further small whorls or pinnacles. It is an attractive plant, with yellowish, lime-green buds.

calabrese broccoli

LEFT Romanesco

COOKING BROCCOLI

Broccoli cooks in no time. Bring a saucepan of lightly salted water to the boil. Add the broccoli and cook for 3–4 minutes until it is just tender.

Kale

Because kale is a leafy, rather than a headed brassica, it is much closer than many of the brassicas in this book to the original wild cabbage, and it is, therefore, probably one of the oldest forms. There are several different types of kale, because the name is used to refer to any leafy brassica, including a whole group of coloured varieties that are used purely as ornamental plants. The main edible group consists of the curly kales, which are also known as borecoles. Another group, particularly popular in the southern United States, is the plain-leaved collards.

Although kale is one of the least popular brassicas as far as culinary uses are concerned, it does fill the period in midwinter when there are few fresh vegetables available, and it is a rich source of vitamins and minerals. Kales are very hardy and withstand winter weather well, and they will also tolerate wet and even poor soil conditions.

The edible varieties are decorative and are often grown for that attribute rather than for their flavour. The leaves of the traditional curly kale are so curled that they look like froth. In recent times the dark, narrow-leaved 'Nero di Toscana' ('Black Tuscany', the palm-tree cabbage) has become popular for its visual qualities, and it is frequently seen in decorative potagers. In addition, there are some non-edible forms that are used purely as decoration both in the kitchen garden and in flower borders. Ornamental kales come in a wonderful range of purples, pinks, reds and creamy-whites. They are at their best in the winter when there is very little else of interest in the garden.

The leaves of kale are eaten, especially the young leaves from the centre of the plant. Part of the resistance to eating kale arises from the fact that some kales are used as cattle and sheep fodder in winter. Some people dislike its strong flavour, which can be rather bitter if the leaves are not cooked properly.

VARIETIES

'Cottagers'
'Dwarf Blue Curled Scotch'
'Dwarf Green Curled'
'Fribor'
'Frosty'
'Hungry Gap'
'Nero di Toscana'
'Pentland Brig'
'Tall Green Curled'
'Thousandhead'

COOKING KALE

Break the leaves from the stalk and cut out any thick stems. Boil the leaves in lightly salted, boiling water for 3–5 minutes until they are just tender. Kale has a strong flavour and is often teamed with spices and used in Indian dishes.

ABOVE Collards

curly kale

Cauliflower

Although they are not the easiest of crops to grow, cauliflowers are one of the most rewarding, both in the sense of achievement they give in the growing and in the pleasure they give in the eating. They are also a good source of vitamin C. Like so many of our vegetables, their origins are rather obscure. The Romans are thought to have cultivated a type of cauliflower, but the vegetable as we know it today originated in the countries at

cauliflower

the eastern end of the Mediterranean at a much later date. It was introduced into Italy in the late 15th century and finally reached Britain about a century later. However, it was another 200 years before it came to be widely grown.

Cauliflowers are characterized by their large, dome-shaped heads of creamy-white flowers, which are generally known as curds. When they are well grown, the curds should be tight, evenly shaped and unblemished. The typical cauliflower has creamy-white curds, but there are also other colours for those who want something a bit different. Purple is the most common alternative colour, but there are also various shades of green and orange, although most of these are not true cauliflowers but hybrids, often produced using broccoli. The heads are usually 15–20cm/6–8in across, but there are now modern hybrids, often known as mini-cauliflowers, which develop very quickly and have heads measuring only 10cm/4in or less across.

There are cauliflowers for almost every season of the year. The only gap comes in winter, because most of the so-called winter cauliflowers are not, in fact, ready until spring.

COOKING CAULIFLOWER

Cauliflower can be boiled with fresh dill, lemon juice, mustard powder and caraway seeds, then puréed to form a satisfying creamy soup. Alternatively, you can stir-fry cauliflower on a high heat with onion and garlic. It is also delicious when simply steamed on its own, or added to cheese sauce for the classic cauliflower cheese.

VARIETIES

Early summer and summer
'All Year Round'
'Alpha'
'Juno'
'Mayflower'
'Montana'
'Snow Crown'
'Snowball A'
'White Summer'

Late summer and autumn
'All Year Round'
'Autumn Glory'
'Castlegrant'
'Dok Elgon'
'Plana'
'Violet Queen'
'Wallaby'

Winter
'Arcade'
'Cappaccio'
'Early Feltham'
'Jerome'
'Purple Cape'

Mini-cauliflowers
'Candid Charm'
'Clarke'
'Mini-Cauliflower King'

BELOW Purple cauliflower

Spinach

Always valued for its nutrients – it is a superb source of beta carotene and fibre – spinach is hated by most children and many adults, and yet when it is cooked properly it is a magnificent vegetable and a key ingredient in many dishes. It is also delicious eaten as raw baby leaves in salads.

Spinach is related to the beetroots (beets) and chards and not to the cabbages or lettuces, to which it bears a superficial resemblance. It was first cultivated in Asia by the Persians, and it spread along the trade routes to China and eventually to Spain by the 11th century.

Spinach is really a plant for a cool climate. It dislikes hot, dry summers, when it will very quickly go to seed, often before it is fully developed and ready to harvest. However, if plants are properly watered and you select cultivars that suit your area, you can produce a crop that should last for two or three weeks and, with successional cropping, this can be extended.

The plants look rather like a loose lettuce, with stalked leaves rising from a central stem. When the plant bolts, this stem quickly elongates. Supplying the plant with plenty of moisture and nourishment can postpone the tendency to bolt.

ALTERNATIVES TO SPINACH

Another vegetable that is cooked in the same way as spinach is New Zealand spinach (*Tetragonia tetragonioides*), which makes a good substitute, both in the garden and kitchen. It is grown as an annual, but unlike true spinach can be picked throughout the summer months and also into autumn.

The young leaves of red orach or red mountain spinach (*Atriplex hortensis*) can also be used in the same way.

spinach

VARIETIES

Summer
'Bloomsdale'
'King of Denmark'
'Long Standing'
'Medana'
'Melody'
'Monopa'
'Triathlon'

Winter
'Broad-leafed Prickly'
'Norvak'
'Sigmaleaf'
'Symphony'

COOKING SPINACH

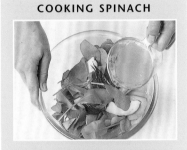

Baby spinach leaves are delicious served raw in a salad. Here, an olive oil dressing is being added to a mixture of spinach, wedges of red onion and avocado slices.

Spinach can be puréed to make a creamy side dish. Rinse and cook spinach leaves in a deep frying pan or wok until wilted. Drain in a colander, then purée in a food processor fitted with a metal blade.

Swiss chard

This vegetable has a number of alternative names, including chard and seakale beet. The red-stemmed forms are known as rhubarb chard, red chard or ruby chard. Spinach beet or perpetual spinach is essentially the same but has thinner stems. All are rich in vitamins and minerals.

Although it is called Swiss chard, the plant originates from around the Mediterranean and dates back long before Switzerland was thought of. Both the Greeks and Romans grew chard, including red-stemmed forms.

Swiss chard

Swiss chard has large, glossy, dark green leaves on wide creamy-white stalks. Both parts can be eaten, although they are often cooked separately, because the stems take much longer than the leaves. Ruby chard is similar, but the stems are a brilliant red and the leaves are a deep purple-green in some varieties and green in others. A third variant are those with striped stems, which can be in a range of colours, including red, yellow and orange. All three versions are decorative and can be used in any ornamental scheme. Unlike some other brightly coloured vegetables – ornamental kale, for example – these chards are eminently edible as well as being attractive.

Perpetual spinach is relatively dull in comparison. It has smaller, less shiny leaves and stems that have no ornamental value at all. However, it makes a very good alternative to spinach and can be used as a straightforward vegetable dish or combined with other ingredients to make something a bit more special.

VARIETIES

Swiss chard
'Argentata' deep green leaves, silvery white stems
'Bright Lights' dark green leaves, red, pink, orange, creamy silver and yellow stems
'Charlotte' purple-red leaves, bright red stems
'Feurio' red leaves, red stems
'Fordhook Giant' deep green leaves, white stems
'Lucullus' pale green, ruffled leaves, white stems
'Rainbow Chard' red, pink, orange, creamy silver or yellow stems.
Sometimes listed simply as 'Beet Swiss Chard' (with white stems) or 'Rhubarb Chard' (with red stems) with no varietal name given.

Perpetual spinach
No cultivars; normally listed as 'perpetual spinach' or 'leaf beet'.

PREPARING SWISS CHARD

Some people buy chard for the white stems alone and discard the leaves, but this is a waste of a delicious vegetable. The leaf needs to be separated from the ribs, and this can be done roughly with a sharp knife or more precisely using scissors. The leaves can then be sliced or used to wrap little parcels of fragrant rice or other food.

ABOVE The vibrant colour of the stems of Swiss chard can be relied on to make a strong decorative statement in the kitchen garden.

Lettuce

The mainstay of salads, lettuce is usually eaten raw, for which home-grown plants are ideal, although an increasing number of recipes feature cooked lettuce. Lettuce leaves are also widely used as a decorative garnish, for which the coloured forms of the loose-leaved varieties are particularly useful. There is now quite a wide range of red- and bronze-leaved lettuces, as well as green forms with attractive leaves. They all contain viatmin C, beta carotene and iron.

The lettuce has been cultivated for thousands of years. In Egyptian times it was sacred to the god Min and was depicted in carvings and paintings in Ancient Egypt. Lettuces were popular among the Romans, too, who are reputed to have introduced them to Britain. The original lettuces were probably quite bitter and needed blanching.

Modern gardeners are fortunate in having so many different types as well as a wide range of varieties to choose from. The main type is the cabbage or headed lettuce. These are either loose balls of soft leaves, butterhead lettuces, or those with much firmer, crinkly-edged leaves, crispheads.

Cos or romaine lettuces are more upright and have long, crisp leaves and a succulent heart. Then there are the loose-leaved or non-heading varieties, which do not produce a heart but just a mass of loose leaves. These lettuces are very good when you want to be able to harvest leaves as and when you require them. There has recently been a great deal of interest in these cut-and-come-again lettuces, and many new varieties have appeared. This method of growing lettuces is far from new, however.

VARIETIES

Butterhead
'Avondefiance'
'Buttercrunch'
'Continuity'
'Dolly'
'Hilde II'
'May King'
'Musette'
'Sabine'
'Tom Thumb'

Crisphead
'Avoncrisp'
'Beatrice'
'Iceberg'
'Lake Nayah'
'Malika'
'Minetto'
'Saladin'
'Warpath'
'Webb's Wonderful'

Cos
'Balloon'
'Bubbles'
'Corsair'
'Little Gem'
'Lobjoits Green Cos'
'Paris White'
'Valmaine'
'Wallop'

Loose-leaved
'Cerise'
'Cocarde'
'Frisby'
'Lollo Rosso'
'Red Fire'
'Red Sails'
'Redina'
'Salad Bowl'

Winter
'Arctic King'
'Kellys'
'Novita'
'Valdor'
'Winter Density'

iceberg lettuce

hearted lettuce

loose-leaved lettuce

cut-and-come-again lettuce

Salad leaves

Although lettuces provide the traditional greenery for most salads, there are an increasing number of small leaves that play their part. Some are available during the winter months, when lettuce from the garden may be scarce. As well as adding bulk to salads, each leaf adds an individual

rocket

flavour to pep up the dish. Like lettuce, salad leaves contain vitamin C, beta carotene and iron.

The two most important of the salad leaves are rocket (also known as salad rocket, rucola, arugula and Italian cress) and lamb's lettuce (also known as corn salad and mâche).

Neither rocket nor lamb's lettuce is new – indeed, both have been cultivated and eaten for centuries – but their popularity seems to be on the increase, particularly in the USA, where numerous varieties are available. The choice of rocket and lamb's lettuce varieties is also increasing in Europe – they have always been particularly popular in France, which is where many of the varieties originate.

Young rocket leaves have a sharp taste, and the older the leaves, the hotter and spicier the taste. They are usually eaten raw in salads, but older leaves are sometimes cooked, and the flowers can be eaten, too.

Lamb's lettuce is used as a winter crop. The leaves are milder than those of rocket, and it is also much slower growing, taking up to 12 weeks before it is ready to cut.

lamb's lettuce

Several alternative salad leaves can be grown, each needing to be cultivated in the same way as rocket and lamb's lettuce. One example is land cress, which tastes like watercress. Mustard and the similar tasting salad rape are also worth growing. Cress, also known as garden or curly cress, can be grown to complement the other leaves, and winter purslane is another mild salad leaf.

PREPARING LETTUCE AND SALAD LEAVES

Pull the leaves away from the stalk, discarding any wilted or damaged leaves. Wash the leaves in plenty of cold water, swirling gently to make sure all the dirt and any insects are washed away.

Place the leaves in a soft dishtowel and gently pat dry. Then wrap in a fresh, dry dishtowel, place in a large plastic bag and chill in the refrigerator for about 1 hour.

planning and
preparation

Growing vegetables is not difficult, as long
as the soil is well prepared and a few
commonsense precautions are taken to protect
young plants and to water them in summer.
Even small gardens have space for a short row
of succulent lettuces or a few crisp cabbages
to provide home-grown produce all year
round. One of the secrets of good vegetable
growing is to make certain that the soil and
the beds are thoroughly prepared. Any time
spent on this will be amply rewarded.
Well-rotted organic material added to the
soil is worth its weight in gold.

Growing in rows

Many vegetables have traditionally been grown in rows. Although some gardeners challenge the claims made for this method, suggesting that blocks and deep beds are better, rows are probably still the most widely used system and are easy to adapt to a range of different plants.

The basic idea is simple: the vegetables are grown in a single line. The lines or rows are separated by a distance somewhat wider than the breadth of the plants, so that there is bare earth between the rows. This bare earth acts as a path, allowing access for maintenance, such as weeding and watering, as well as for harvesting. Apart from good horticultural practice, there is something rather satisfying and aesthetically pleasurable about seeing vegetables spread out in neat rows.

ADVANTAGES

Growing vegetables in rows is an attractive way of producing them. The varying heights, shapes, textures and colours show up well, with the rows looking like decorative ribbons stretched across the garden. Their appearance is not, however, the principal reason for growing vegetables in this way. There are practical considerations, too.

Access is one of the important benefits provided by individual rows. The paths between the rows allow the gardener to move freely among the plants without having to stretch. Each plant can be examined for condition as well as for pests and diseases. Pests have less chance of being overlooked if the plant can be clearly seen from at least two sides, and individual plants can be attended to if it becomes necessary. The bases

ABOVE Spinach grows best in short rows rather than one long one.

of the plants are exposed for inspection, weeding and watering.

Another advantage is that plenty of air can circulate among the plants, which helps to reduce mildew-type diseases. The plants generally have plenty of space in which to develop, and the leaves are able to open out to receive the

BELOW Neat rows are the most popular way of growing vegetables.

maximum amount of light. Finally, rows are easy to cover with the majority of cloches available.

DISADVANTAGES

Needless to say there are also disadvantages. Allowing for walkways between rows of vegetables means that nearly half of the plot is not producing crops. This is an important factor in a small garden, where the space that can be devoted to vegetables is limited.

Another disadvantage is that the paths allow light to reach the soil, so increasing the number of weeds that germinate, although this is offset to some extent by the ease

with which it is possible to hoe. With constant use, the paths become compacted, which does not help the soil structure.

Although the whole bed will be dug each year, because it is so large it will be necessary to walk over it while the ground is being prepared, again adding a certain degree of compaction. Constant hoeing will help to overcome this by breaking up the soil and keeping it aerated. However, in dry weather, hoeing should be avoided because it encourages water loss. An alternative is to lay planks of wood between the rows. This not only helps to prevent soil compaction

ABOVE It is important to leave plenty of room for young plants to fill out. Rows with plenty of space between them also allow for access and easy weeding.

but also acts as a type of mulch, which will help to retain moisture in the soil and keep weeds down.

Laying organic mulch such as straw or grass cuttings also helps to a certain extent with the compaction problem. Such a mulch is, of course, also useful for keeping down the weeds and preventing the moisture from evaporating from the soil. Dig the mulch in at the end of the growing season.

Growing in blocks

Planting vegetables in blocks as opposed to rows is an old method that has become popular again in recent years. The basic idea is to grow the plants in a square or rectangle, say five plants wide by five plants deep, rather than in a single row.

DIVIDING THE PLOT

The vegetable plot is divided into smaller plots, each about 1.2m/4ft across and spanning the width of the main plot. These smaller beds are permanent, and between each is a path of trodden earth or paving slabs or bricks. The width of the smaller beds is determined by the gardener's reach – 1.2m/4ft should allow access of about 60cm/24in from each side so that the entire bed can be reached.

Some gardeners simply dig the soil in the existing plot, adding organic material to it as they go.

Others prefer to create a deep bed system, by digging deeper, by using a double digging method or by raising the height of the bed with boards or a low wall and adding a mixture of loam and organic material. The bed is worked from the path, so that the soil never becomes compacted.

A good depth of rich, fertile soil means that plants can be grown more closely together than in the conventional rows, thus increasing productivity for a given area. As well as being productive, close planting also means that weed seeds have little chance of germinating.

DISADVANTAGES

A solid block of plants makes it more difficult to get at any weeds, as well as making it harder to see if there are any pests and diseases lurking below the leaves. Because

ABOVE These blocks of contrasting lettuces have been planted in deep beds that are almost flush with the ground. The beds have been dug deeply rather than built up.

the plants are close together, there is likely to be less air circulating than around vegetables grown in rows, and this increases the possibility of diseases that like damp conditions. It is also not as easy to water the base of individual plants, and watering can become erratic, with some areas ending up drier than others as water runs off the leaves. Another disadvantage is that it is not as easy to cover the vegetables with cloches, and although it is possible to construct a cover, this will not be as mobile as individual cloches.

LEFT Raised beds improve drainage and help a soil to warm up more quickly in spring, as well as creating a deep layer of fertile soil, allowing for closer planting.

Growing in containers

Increasing interest is being shown in containers as a method of growing a few vegetables in a small space, perhaps on the patio or possibly even on a balcony or roof garden. A wide range of beautiful containers are now available from garden centres and nurseries, many of which will accommodate greens.

THE CONTAINERS

Virtually any container can be used to grow vegetables, but success is more likely if it is reasonably large – the bigger the better, in fact. Most vegetables do not like to dry out, and the greater the volume of compost (soil mix) that is available, the less chance there is of this happening. A larger amount of space also allows you to grow several different plants in the same container, which is much more decorative than using just one type.

Terracotta pots are attractive, but the porous nature of the material allows water to evaporate more quickly through the sides of the pot than through, say, a glazed one. Most pots are heavy even without compost (soil mix), so make sure you position them before you fill them. Large plastic buckets with drainage holes are practical and can be used successfully, although they are not as attractive as ceramic pots.

GROWING BAGS

If you do not mind their utilitarian appearance, growing bags – plastic sacks filled with a formulated growing medium – are an inexpensive way of growing vegetables. They are particularly useful for plants such as tomatoes, but they can be used for many other vegetables as well. They were originally developed for use in the greenhouse (where their appearance does not matter), but they can be used outside just as well. A warm corner, against a wall, is the ideal location.

HANGING BASKETS

Most vegetables are not suitable for hanging baskets, mainly because they are too small to allow a good root run, but a basket of decorative lettuces, perhaps a mixture of green and bronze varieties, can be eye-catching. A little imagination should allow you to create something productive as well as attractive, although regular watering is essential. Pick leaves carefully to maintain the display.

THE POSITION

Containers of vegetables can be placed together with purely decorative containers, although they should not be grown in shade. Unlike fruit-bearing plants, like tomatoes and peppers for example, most greens prefer not to get too hot – after all, they even grow in autumn and winter.

You should bear in mind that plants grown in pots do not have the solid mass of earth around their roots to keep them cool during the day, and it is possible that the roots can become too hot. Another problem with siting the containers in a warm place is that they will need watering several times a day.

BELOW Cabbage may not be the first planting idea that springs to mind when thinking of containers, but here four good specimens are growing happily in a large plastic tub.

Intercropping

There can be few gardeners who have enough space to grow everything they wish, and those with small gardens often struggle to find any space for vegetables. One way partly to overcome the problem is to make sure that every available piece of land is in use and to avoid letting ground lie idle.

USING SPACE

There are two main ways to ensure that the land is used efficiently. The first is to plant quick-growing crops among slower ones so that the former have been harvested before the latter have grown sufficiently to fill the space. Brussels sprouts, for example, are planted at anything up to 75cm/30in apart, depending on the size of the variety. For several weeks after they have been planted there is a lot of empty space around each plant. This can be filled with a crop such as lettuce or spinach that takes only a short while to come to maturity.

Some plants, however, cannot be planted out in the early part of the season, and rather than leave the ground empty, it can be filled with a temporary crop. For example, a bed of lettuces can be planted and the first ones to be harvested can be replaced by mizuna greens, the rest of the lettuces being harvested as the greens develop.

A similar idea can be used with station-sown seeds. For example, parsnip seeds can be sown in groups of three at, say, 23cm/9in intervals. In between each group a few radishes can be sown. This method has advantages in that not only will the quick-growing radishes make use of the ground before the parsnips need it, but, because parsnips are slow to germinate, the radishes will actually mark the row, making it easier to hoe off any weeds without disturbing the parsnips, which are still below ground.

COLOURFUL CROPS

Another aspect of intercropping is purely decorative. A simple example is to intercrop red-leaved lettuces with green ones. To create these effects, it is best to raise the plants in trays or modules and plant them out in a pattern when they are large enough.

When you are intercropping for visual effects, take care in the choice of neighbours. There is little point in planting decorative cabbages next to spinach, which will eventually overwhelm and smother them. However, from the productive point of view it is a good idea to plant cabbages between rows of spinach before the latter have emerged or have reached any height, because the cabbages will be cropped before the ground is overshadowed by the spinach. In decorative potager gardens it is possible to keep a few young plants in pots as replacements for when crops are harvested.

ABOVE Quick-growing crops such as spinach can be grown between cabbages. They will crop long before the cabbages have grown large enough to cover them.

ABOVE As an alternative to growing lettuces on their own, they can be planted between slow-growing plants such as cabbages.

Successional crops

One of the great benefits of growing green vegetables in your own garden is that it is possible to select a range of types and cultivars that will give a supply of fresh produce over a long period. In addition to choosing vegetables that crop over an extended period, it is possible to sow in succession so that the same vegetables do not all appear at the same time. By spreading the harvesting period, you can avoid summer gluts and shortages in autumn and winter.

SHORT ROWS

Many gardeners tend to sow a complete row right across the plot, whether they need that amount of produce or not, either because they think that a whole row looks better than a short one or because they want to finish off a packet of seeds. This can be wasteful, because it is quite likely that about two-thirds of the row will bolt before you have time to eat it and it will have to be thrown away. It is far better to sow, say, a third of the row, then to wait two or three weeks and sow another third of the row, and to wait another two or three weeks before sowing to the end of the row. A good rule is to sow the next batch of seed just as the previous sowing is beginning to emerge as seedlings, with their first leaves.

This approach will mean that crops will reach maturity at two- or three-week intervals, so that you have the vegetable for two months or more rather than for the two or

three weeks that would have been the case if you had sown the whole row at once.

Among the most appropriate vegetables for sowing in this way are fairly fast-growing crops like spinach, calabrese broccoli, lettuce, corn salad and rocket.

CHOOSING CULTIVARS

In addition to delaying sowing, it is possible to select cultivars of plants that will crop at different times of year. Cabbage, for example, can be available all year round if you are prepared to select a number of different cultivars. Cabbage for cropping in spring and early summer can be sown towards the end of summer and planted out in early autumn. Summer cabbage, sown in mid- or late spring and planted out in early summer, can be harvested in late summer and early autumn, and winter cabbage, sown in mid- to late spring and

ABOVE Some crops are better planted at intervals so that they do not all mature at the same time. To facilitate this, it is often easier to fill long rows with several different types of vegetables rather than leave gaps to be sown later. The method is decorative as well as practical.

planted out in midsummer, will be ready for harvesting from late autumn until late winter.

Other vegetables that have a range of cultivars for different seasons include lettuce and cauliflower. Some cultivars are even specifically labelled as quick- or early-cropping, and these are invaluable for the beginning and end of the season.

There may, of course, be times when you do not want to spread the harvesting. If, for example, you like to freeze vegetables for winter use it is easier if they all mature at once so that you can freeze them in batches and use the ground for something else.

Types of soil

Vegetables can, within reason, be grown on most soils, but, as one would expect, there is an optimum soil in which the best vegetables can be grown. Most soils can be persuaded, with varying degrees of effort, to move towards that optimum, but the starting point is often different.

CLAY

When they work well clay soils can be fertile, but their structure is the despair of most gardeners. Clay is heavy, and the particles cling together, making the soil sticky. Clay soil compacts easily, forming a solid lump that roots find hard to penetrate and that is difficult to dig. Try not to walk on clay soils when they are wet. They are slow to drain, but, once drained, they "set" like concrete, becoming a hard mass.

Clay soil is not, one would think, suitable for growing vegetables, yet many of the best gardens are on clay. The soils are usually rich, and the hard work needed in the initial stages pays off in the long term.

SANDY SOILS

Soils that are made up of sand and silts are quite different to clay soils. Sandy soils have few of the sticky clay particles but are made up of individual grains that allow the water to pass through quickly. This quick passage of water through the soil tends to leach (wash) out nutrients, so the soil is often poor. But it also tends to be much warmer in winter and is quicker to warm up in spring, thus making it easier to get early crops.

Silts contain particles that are rather more clay-like in structure, allowing them to hold slightly more moisture and more nutrients than sandy soils.

Both types of soil are easy to improve and are not difficult to work. Sand does not compact like clay does (although it is still not good practice to walk on beds), but silty soils are more susceptible to the impact of feet.

LOAMS

The soil of most gardeners' dreams is loam. This is a combination of clay and sandy soils, with the best elements of both. They tend to be free-draining, but at the same time moisture-retentive. This description – free-draining and moisture-retentive – is often used of soils and potting mixes, and it may seem a contradiction. It means that the soil is sufficiently free-draining to allow excess moisture to drain away, but enough moisture is retained for the plant without it standing in stagnant water. Such soils are easy to work at any time of the year, and they warm up well in spring and are thus good for early crops.

ACID AND ALKALINE SOILS

Another way of classifying soils is by their acidity or alkalinity. Those that are based on peat (peat moss) are acid; those that include chalk or limestone are alkaline. Gardeners use a scale of pH levels to indicate the degree of acidity or alkalinity. Very acid is 1, neutral is 7 and very alkaline is 14, although soils rarely have values at the extremes of the

TESTING SOIL FOR NUTRIENTS

1 Collect the soil sample 5–8cm/2–3in below the surface. Take a number of samples, but test each one separately.

2 With this kit, mix one part of soil with five parts of water. Shake well in a jar, then allow the water to settle.

3 Draw off some of the settled liquid from the top few centimetres (about an inch) for your test.

4 Carefully transfer the solution to the test chamber in the plastic container, using the pipette.

5 Select a colour-coded capsule (one for each nutrient). Put the powder in the chamber, replace the cap and shake well.

6 After a few minutes, compare the colour of the liquid with the panel on the container.

scale. Vegetables can be grown on a wide range of soils, but the best pH for them is slightly on the acid side of neutral; they are usually grown in soils with a pH of 5.5–7.5, with the optimum conditions being around 6.5. A test with a soil kit will show the rating in your garden. You can adjust acid soils, but it is more difficult to alter the pH of alkaline ones.

IMPROVING THE SOIL'S PH

If the soil is too acid, the pH can be adjusted somewhat by adding lime to the soil. Ordinary lime (calcium carbonate) is the safest to use. Quicklime (calcium oxide) is the strongest and most caustic. Slaked lime (calcium hydroxide, quicklime with water added) is not as strong as quicklime and is therefore not so dangerous.

Always take safety precautions when you apply lime and follow the quantities recommended by the manufacturer. Do not add lime at the same time as manure, because this will release ammonia, which can damage the plants. Spread the lime over the soil at the rate prescribed on the packet and rake it in. Do not sow or plant in the ground for at least a month. Do not over-lime.

IMPROVING SOIL QUALITY

Perhaps the most important task in any garden is to improve and maintain the quality of the soil. Good-quality soil should be the aim of any gardener who wants to grow vegetables or fruit. To ignore the soil is to ignore one of the garden's most important assets.

The key to improving the soil in your garden is organic material. This is an all-embracing term that covers any vegetable matter that has been broken down into an odourless, fibrous compost. It includes such things as rotted garden waste, kitchen vegetable waste, farmyard manures (which are plant materials that have passed through animals) and other plant waste material.

It is important that this material is well-rotted. If it is still in the process of breaking down, it will extract nitrogen from the soil to complete the process. This, of course, is the reverse of what the gardener wants – the gardener's aim is to add nitrogen to the soil. If you are unsure, a good indicator that the material has broken down sufficiently is that it is odourless. Even rotted horse manure is free from odour, and manuring a garden should not be a smelly occupation.

Some substances contain undesirable chemicals, but these will be removed if the material is stacked and allowed to weather. Bark and other shredded woody materials may contain resins, while animal and bird manures may contain ammonia from urea. These chemicals will evaporate or be converted by weathering.

REDUCING SOIL ACIDITY

The acidity of the soil can be reduced by adding lime some weeks before planting and working it in with a rake. Check the soil with a soil testing kit to see how much lime is required.

IMPROVING SOIL FERTILITY

The fertility of the soil is much improved by the addition of organic material, but a quick boost can be achieved by adding an organic fertilizer, spreading it over the surface and raking it in.

Soil conditioners

A wide range of organic soil conditioners are available to the gardener. Some are free – if you do not count the time taken in working and carting them. Others are relatively cheap, and some, usually those bought by the bag, can be quite expensive. However, not everyone has a stable nearby or enough space to store large quantities of material, and many gardeners will therefore need to buy it as required.

FARMYARD MANURE

A traditional material and still much used by many country gardeners, farmyard manure has the advantage of adding bulk to the soil as well as supplying valuable nutrients. The manure can come from any form of livestock, although the most commonly available is horse manure. It can be obtained from most stables, and many are so glad to get rid of it that they will supply it free if you fetch it yourself. There are often stables situated around the edge of towns, so manure is usually available to town gardeners as well as to those in the country.

Some gardeners do not like the manure when it is mixed with wood shavings rather than with straw, but it is worth bearing in mind that the former is often less likely to contain weed seeds, and as long as it is stacked and allowed to rot down it is excellent for adding to the soil as well as for use as a top-dressing.

All manures should be stacked for a period of at least six months before they are used. When the manure is ready to use, it will have lost its dungy smell.

GARDEN COMPOST

All gardeners should make an effort to recycle as much of their garden and kitchen vegetable waste as possible. In essence, this is simply following nature's pattern, where leaves and stems are formed in the spring and die back in the autumn, falling to the ground and eventually

ABOVE Green manure helps to improve both the structure and fertility of the soil. Sow it when the ground is not being used for anything else and then dig it in before it flowers and sets seed.

rotting and returning to the plants as nutrients. In the garden some things are removed from the cycle, notably vegetables and fruit, but as much as possible should be returned to the earth.

Compost is not difficult to make, and, of course, it is absolutely free. If you have the space, use several bins at the same time, so there is always some that is ready for use.

Unless weeds that are in seed or diseased plants have been used, compost should be safe to use as a soil conditioner and as a mulch.

LEAF MOULD

Leaf mould is a natural soil conditioner. It is easy to make and should not cost anything. Only use

ORGANIC MATERIALS

well-rotted farmyard manure

well-rotted garden compost

leaf mould made by yourself; never go down to the local woods and help yourself because this will disturb the wood's own cycle and will impoverish the soil there.

Four stakes knocked into the ground with a piece of wire netting stretched around them will make the perfect container for making leaf mould. Simply add the leaves as they fall from the trees. It will take a couple of years for them to break down and what was a huge heap will shrink to a small layer by the time the process is complete.

Add leaf mould to the soil or use it as a top-dressing. It is usually acid and can be used to reduce the pH of alkaline soil. Leaf mould resulting from pine needles is particularly acid.

PEAT (PEAT MOSS)

This is expensive and does little for the soil because it breaks down too quickly and has little nutritive content. However, the reasons for not using it have nothing to do with its nutritional content. Peat (peat moss) is taken from bogs, rare and fragile ecosystems that are rapidly being depleted. Gardeners do not need to use peat and should always look for environmentally responsible alternatives.

SPENT MUSHROOM COMPOST

Often available locally from mushroom farms, the spent compost is relatively cheap, especially if it is purchased in bulk. It is mainly used in the ornamental part of the garden, but it is still useful in the vegetable garden if it is allowed to rot down. You should allow for the fact that it contains chalk, and so will increase the alkalinity of the soil.

VEGETABLE INDUSTRIAL WASTE

Several industries produce organic waste material that can be useful in the garden. Spent hop waste from the brewing industry is a

favourite among those who can obtain it. Cocoa shells are now imported, although these are better used as a mulch than as a soil conditioner. They are comparatively high in nitrogen. Several other products are locally available. Allow them to rot well before using.

GREEN MANURE

Some crops can be grown simply to be dug back into the ground, so as to improve the soil condition and to add nutrients. They are useful on light soils that are vacant for any length of time, such as over winter. Green manures can be sown in early autumn and dug in during spring.

WORKING IN ORGANIC MATTER

1 Soil that has been dug in the autumn can have more organic matter worked into the top layer in the spring. Spread the organic matter over the surface.

2 Lightly work the organic material into the top layer of soil with a fork. There is no need for full-scale digging.

Making compost

Compost is a valuable material for any garden, but it is especially useful in the vegetable garden. It is free, apart from any capital spent on installing bins. You can apply compost to a vegetable plot in spring or summer as a mulch, or dig it into the top 20cm/8in of the soil.

THE PRINCIPLE

The idea behind compost-making is to emulate the process in which a plant takes nutrients from the soil, dies and then rots, putting the nutrients back into the ground. In the garden, waste plant material is collected, piled in a heap and allowed to rot down before being returned to the soil as crumbly, sweet-smelling, fibrous material.

Because it is in a heap, the rotting material generates heat, which encourages it to break down even more quickly. The heat also helps to kill pests and diseases and any weed seed. A certain amount of moisture is needed, as well as air. If there is too much water, the process is slowed down; if there is insufficient air, the heap will go slimy and smell bad.

The process should take up to about three months, but some gardeners like to retain the heap for much longer, growing marrows and the like on it before they use it in the garden.

THE COMPOST BIN

Gardeners always seem to generate more garden waste than they ever thought possible and never have enough compost space, so when planning your bins, make sure you have enough. The ideal is to have three bins: one for new waste, one that is in the process of breaking down, and a third that is ready for using on the garden.

A standard dustbin (trash can) is the minimum size to enable the compost to heat up adequately, but if you have room, a cubic metre/35 cubic feet or even twice this size

ABOVE A range of organic materials can be used, but avoid cooked kitchen waste or any weeds that have seed in them. Clockwise from top left: kitchen waste, weeds, shreddings and grass clippings.

would be more efficient. The simplest bin can be made by nailing together four wooden pallets to form a box. If the front is made so that the slats are slotted in to form the wall, they can be removed as the bin is emptied, making the job of removing the compost easier.

MATERIALS

Most garden plant waste can be used for composting as long as it does not contain weed seeds. You should also avoid including perennial weeds or diseased plants. Woody material, such as hedge clippings, should be shredded

LEFT Only a small proportion of the vegetables and flowers in this plot will be used. This means that most of the foliage and stems can be put in the compost bin.

before adding to the compost bin. It is advisable not to use evergreen such as fir or holly. Kitchen vegetable waste, such as peelings and cores, can be used, but avoid cooked vegetables, and do not include animal products, which will attract rats and other vermin.

TECHNIQUE

Place a few branches or twiggy material in the bottom to keep the contents aerated. Put in the material as it becomes available but avoid building up deep layers of any one material, especially grass cuttings.

To help keep the heap warm, cover it with an old carpet or sheet of polythene (plastic). This also prevents excess water from chilling the contents as well as swamping all the air spaces. The lid should be kept on until the compost is required.

Every so often, add a layer of farmyard manure if you can get it to provide extra nitrogen to speed things up, or add a proprietary compost accelerator. This is not essential, however.

Air is important, and this usually percolates through the side of the bin, so leave a few gaps between the timbers. The colder material around the edges takes longer to break down than that in the centre of the heap, so turn the compost every so often. This also loosens the pile and allows air to circulate.

MAKING COMPOST

1 A simple compost bin can be made by nailing four flat pallets together. If the bin is roughly made, this will ensure that there will be plenty of air holes between the slats.

2 Pile in the waste, making certain that there are no thick layers of the same material. Grass clippings will not rot down if the layer is too thick because the air cannot penetrate.

3 Keep the compost covered with an old mat or a sheet of polythene (sheet vinyl or plastic) to keep in the heat generated by the rotting process and stop the compost from getting too wet when it rains.

4 Every so often turn the compost with a fork to let in air and to move the outside material, which is slow to rot, into the centre to speed up the process. It is easier if you have several bins and turn the compost from one bin into another.

5 When the bin is full, cover the surface with a layer of soil and use it to grow marrows (zucchini), pumpkins or cucumbers. If you want to use the contents as soon as possible, omit the soil and keep covered with polythene.

ABOVE The finished product is dark brown and crumbly and has a sweet, earthy smell, not a rotting one. It can be used straight away or left covered until it is required.

Fertilizers

You cannot go on taking things out of the soil without putting anything back. In nature plants return the nutrients they have taken from the soil when they die. In the garden the vegetables are removed and the chain is broken. Compost and other organic materials help to redress the balance, but there may not be enough to do the job properly and then fertilizers are needed, applied at regular intervals.

WHAT PLANTS REQUIRE

The main foods required by plants are nitrogen (N), phosphorus (P) and potassium (K), with smaller quantities of magnesium (Mg), calcium (Ca) and sulphur (S). They also require small amounts of trace elements, including iron (Fe) and manganese (Mn).

Each of the main nutrients is used by the plant for one specific function. Nitrogen is concerned with plant growth and used for promoting the rapid growth of the green parts of the plant. Phosphorus, usually in the form of phosphates, is used to create good root growth as well as helping with the ripening of fruits, while potassium, in the form of potash, is used to promote flowering and formation of good fruit.

ORGANIC FERTILIZERS

Concentrated fertilizers are of two types: organic and inorganic. Organic fertilizers consist solely of naturally occurring materials and contain different proportions of nutrients. So bonemeal (ground-up bones), which is strong in phosphates and nitrogen, promotes growth, especially root growth. Bonemeal also has the advantage that it breaks down slowly, gradually releasing the fertilizer over a long period. (Wear gloves when you apply bonemeal.)

Other organic fertilizers include fish, blood and bone (high in nitrogen and phosphates); hoof and horn (nitrogen); and seaweed meal (nitrogen and potash). Because they are derived from natural products without any modification, they are used by organic growers.

INORGANIC FERTILIZERS

These are fertilizers that have been made artificially, although they are frequently derived from natural rocks and minerals and the process may just involve crushing. They are concentrated and are usually soluble in water. This means that they are instantly available for the plant. They do, however, tend to wash out of the soil quickly and need to be replaced.

Some are general fertilizers, and might contain equal proportions of nitrogen, phosphorus and potassium. Others are specific: superphosphate, for example, is entirely used for supplying phosphorus, while potassium sulphate is added when extra potassium is required.

SLOW-RELEASE FERTILIZERS

A modern trend is to coat the fertilizers so that they are released slowly into the soil. These are expensive in the short term, but because they do not leach away and do not need to be replaced as frequently, they are more economic in the longer term.

They are particularly useful for container planting, where constant watering is necessary which dissolves and washes away normal fertilizer.

ORGANIC FERTILIZERS

blood

bonemeal

seaweed

fish/blood/bone

INORGANIC FERTILIZERS

Growmore (not available in USA)

sulphate of ammonia

potash

superphosphate

Digging soil

Although some gardeners question its value, winter digging – when there are no crops in the soil – is still an important activity. It breaks up the soil, allowing in water and air, which are important for plant growth. It also allows organic material to be incorporated deep in the soil, right where the roots need it. All weeds and their roots can be removed during digging. It also enables the gardener to spot the more visible types of pest, and destroy any that come to the surface.

1 Divide the space to be dug in half lengthways, marking the area with string. Dividing the plot like this avoids moving excavated soil from one end of the plot to the other.

2 Take out a trench the depth and width of a spade blade. Pile the soil at the end of the other half of the plot, as shown, using a wheelbarrow if necessary.

3 When you remove the next trench, throw the soil forward into the space left by the first. Begin by cutting a slice the width of the bite of soil to be dug.

4 Push the spade in parallel to the trench, taking a slice of soil 15–20cm/6–8in deep. Larger bites may be too heavy to lift comfortably.

5 Loosen the soil by pulling back on the handle, while trying to keep the bite of soil on the spade. Take care that you do not strain your back.

6 Flick the soil over with the wrist, inverting the clod of earth so that the top is buried.

7 When the end of the plot is reached, fill the trench with soil taken from the first row of the return strip.

8 Finally, fill the trench left when digging has been completed with the soil put on one side from the initial excavation.

Sowing in the open

Most vegetables and herbs can be sown directly into the open ground. The two main advantages of doing this are that no indoor facilities are required and the plants' growth is not delayed by planting them out. Some plants resent their roots being disturbed when they are transplanted.

SOIL REQUIREMENTS

The main requirement is that the soil should be broken down into a fine tilth – in other words, the soil crumbs should be small. The soil should be neither too wet nor too dry. If it is wet, cover it with cloches or sheets of polythene (plastic) to prevent it being further wetted and wait until it dries out a little before sowing. If the soil is too dry, water the ground a short time before sowing; there should be sufficient water to soak in but not leave a sticky surface. The ground should also be warm. Seeds sown in cold ground will frequently just sit there until they rot. Ideally, the soil should be at a temperature of at least 7°C/45°F.

SEED REQUIREMENTS

Most of the seed that is available these days is of a high quality, especially when it comes from the major suppliers. The germination rate is usually good, although occasionally an unsatisfactory batch gets through the system. Non-germination may occur, but this is usually due to some other factor, such as cold conditions. It is possible to keep your own seed, but only do this for non-F1 hybrids because F1s will not come true to type. Most seed is sold loose in packets, but seeds can be bought in other forms, and one of the most common is pelleted, when the seeds are coated with clay. The coating makes the seeds easier to handle and to sow. Increasingly,

ABOVE Some seed benefits from an hour's soaking in tepid water before it is sown.

pre-germinated seeds and young seedlings are also becoming available. For most purposes, however, ordinary seeds will be suitable and certainly the cheapest.

SOWING IN ROWS

The conventional way of sowing seeds is to do so in rows. Using a garden line for guidance, draw out a shallow drill in the fine soil with the corner of a hoe. If the ground is dry, water along the drill with a fine-rose watering can. Sow the seeds thinly. Mark the ends of the row with a label and a stick and draw the soil back over the drill with a rake. The depth of the drill should depend on the size of the seeds, but most finer seeds can be sown at a depth of 1cm/½in. The seed packet usually gives an indication of the depth required.

LEFT Vegetables that are usually planted out, rather than sown where they are to grow, such as these cabbages, can still be sown in the open and then transplanted when they are large enough.

STATION SOWING

With plants that grow quite large and therefore need to be spaced out in the row, it is wasteful to sow a continuous line of seeds. Station sowing involves sowing three seeds at distances that will be the eventual gap between plants.

WIDE ROWS

Some seeds, such as some lettuces, are sown in wide rows – in effect, two rows are sown at once. A wide drill, 15cm/6in across, is made with the flat of the hoe. Two rows of seed are sown, one down each side of the drill, and the soil is carefully raked back over the seeds so that they are not disturbed.

BROADCASTING

This is the best method for sowing seeds in blocks. Rake the area to a fine tilth and scatter the seeds thinly but evenly over the surface. If the soil is dry, gently rake the seeds in and water with a fine-rose watering can.

PROTECTING

Fine earth is attractive to both birds and animals as a dust bath as well as a litter tray, and when it is used the seeds will be scattered far and wide. In addition, some birds find emerging seedlings an irresistible source of food. Protect the seeds by placing wire netting guards along the rows. Alternatively, a few pea-sticks can be laid across the surface of the soil. Another possibility is to place short sticks in the ground and to twine cotton thread between them. This last method is the least convenient because the protection cannot be quickly removed and replaced to permit for hoeing and weeding.

Finally, remember to label the rows of seeds, so that you do not inadvertently disturb them.

SOWING SEED

1 Draw out a shallow drill with the corner of a draw hoe, using a garden line to ensure that it is straight.

2 If the soil is dry, water along the length of the drill and allow it to drain before sowing seed.

3 Sow the seed along the drill, sowing it as thinly as possible to reduce the amount of thinning necessary.

4 Put a label at the end of the row clearly showing what is in the row. Put a stick or another label at the far end. Do this before filling in the drill.

5 Rake the soil into the drill over the seed. Gently tamp down the soil along the row with the flat of the rake and then lightly rake over.

6 If the soil is heavy and is difficult to break into a fine tilth, draw out the drill and then line it with potting compost (soil mix) before sowing the seed.

Sowing under glass

Germinating seeds under glass is more tedious and time-consuming than sowing directly into the ground, but raising plants in this way allows the gardener to grow plants that have already reached a reasonable size by the time the weather is warm enough to plant them out, thus enabling a harvest about two weeks earlier. Plants are better able to resist pests, such as slugs or birds, if they are well grown when they are planted out than if they have to fight for their life as soon as they emerge through the soil.

CONTAINERS

Seeds can be sown in a variety of containers. Traditionally, they were sown in wooden trays or flats, but plastic trays have generally replaced the wooden varieties. They can be made of rigid plastic for repeated use or thin, flimsy plastic, to be used only once before being thrown away. Often, only a few plants may be required, and it is rather wasteful to sow a whole or half tray. In this case, a 9cm/3½in pot is usually sufficient.

More and more gardeners are using modular or cellular trays, in which one or two seeds are sown in a small cell. If both the seeds germinate, one is removed and the remaining seedling is allowed to develop without having to be pricked out. This method avoids a lot of root disturbance.

Even less root disturbance occurs if the seeds are sown in

individual biodegradable fibrous modules. As soon as the seedling is big enough to be planted out, both pot and plant are inserted into the ground, and the pot allows the roots to grow through its sides into the surrounding earth and eventually rots away.

SOWING IN BLOCKS

Fill the cellular block with compost (soil mix) and tap it on the table to firm it down. Sow one or two seeds in each cell. Cover with a light dusting of compost. Remove the weaker of the two seedlings after germination.

SOWING IN TRAYS

1 Fill the seed tray with seed compost and tamp down the compost lightly to produce a level surface. Sow the seed thinly and evenly across the surface of the compost.

PROPAGATORS

Propagators are glass or plastic boxes that help to keep the seed tray moist and in a warm atmosphere. The more expensive models have heating cables so that the temperature can be controlled. Although they are desirable, they

SOWING IN POTS

Fill the pot with a good seed compost, tap it on the bench and sow one to three seeds in each pot. Once germinated, the weaker seedlings will be removed, leaving one to grow on.

2 Cover the seeds with a thin layer of compost, lightly firm down and label. Labelling is very important because the seedlings of many vegetables look exactly the same.

WATERING IN

Water the trays or pots by standing them in a shallow tray of water so that the water comes halfway up the container. Remove the tray or pot as soon as the surface of the compost is moist.

are by no means essential. A cheap alternative can be made simply by slipping the tray into a plastic bag and removing it as soon as the seeds have germinated.

HEAT

A source of heat is useful for rapid germination. It can be provided in the form of a heated propagator, but most seeds will germinate in the ambient temperature of a warm greenhouse or conservatory, or even within the house.

SOWING SEED

Fill the seed tray with a good quality seed or potting compost (soil mix). Gently firm down and sow the seeds thinly on the surface. Spread a thin layer of potting compost over the seeds so that they are just covered. Again, firm down lightly. Water by placing the seed tray in a shallow bowl of water, so that the level of the water comes halfway up the sides of the seed tray. Once the surface of the

USING A PROPAGATOR

1 Place the trays or pots in a propagator. You can adjust the temperature of heated propagators like this, but you may need to compromise if different seeds need different temperatures.

compost looks damp, remove the tray and place it in a propagator or in a plastic bag.

SUBSEQUENT TREATMENT

As soon as the seeds begin to germinate, remove the lid from the propagator or open the bag to let in air and after a couple of days remove the tray altogether. If you are using a propagator, turn off the heat and open the vents over a few days and then remove the tray.

USING A COLD FRAME

1 Once the trays of seedlings are ready to plant out, harden them off by placing them in a cold frame, which is opened a little wider each day to let in more air.

2 This unheated propagator should be kept in a warm position in a greenhouse or in the house. Start opening the vents once the seeds have germinated to begin the hardening-off process.

Once the seedlings are large enough to handle, prick them out into trays, individual pots or modules. Hold the seedlings by the seed-leaves and not by the stem or roots. Make sure they are well spaced in the trays and keep them warm and watered.

As the time approaches to plant them out, harden them off by exposing them to outdoor conditions for a little longer each day until they can be safely left out overnight.

2 Finally, leave the lights of the cold frame off altogether so that the plants can become accustomed to the outside temperature.

Thinning and transplanting

Outdoor-sown seedlings inevitably grow too thickly, no matter how thinly you try to sow them. In order to grow properly, they will need thinning. Seeds are often sown in a row that will not be their ultimate cropping position. Kale, for example, can be grown in a seed row and later transplanted to its final position.

WHY THIN?

It is important that vegetables have enough space in which to develop. Plants that are too close together become drawn as they try to move to the light. In addition to not having room to develop, they become undernourished as they compete with their neighbours for moisture, nutrients and light. Crops that are too tightly planted are more susceptible to disease because air cannot circulate freely around them, allowing fungal diseases, such as mildew, to get a hold. Half-starved plants are also more prone to disease than fully nourished ones. A little attention at this stage will pay dividends in producing healthy plants.

THINNING AND TRANSPLANTING SEEDLINGS

1 Water the row of seedlings, the night before if possible, but at least a few hours before transplanting.

2 Using a hand fork, dig up, rather than pull out, the excess plants. Only dig up the plants as you need them; do not dig them up all at once and leave them lying around.

3 Using a garden line to keep the row straight, and a measuring stick to get the distances equal, replant the seedlings using a trowel.

4 Gently firm in each plant and water around them. Rake the soil around the plants in order to tidy it up and to remove footprints and uneven soil.

THINNING

The idea behind thinning is to remove all unwanted plants, leaving the best at regular intervals. Before you begin to thin, water the row to soften the earth and to make sure that the remaining plants have taken up enough water in case their roots are accidentally disturbed. Allow the water to soak in and the plants to take it up. If possible, water the evening before you plan to thin.

Go along the row, with a measuring stick if you are uncertain about the distances between the plants, removing the weaker seedlings and leaving one strong one at the correct planting distance for that particular variety – 15–23cm/6–9in for calabrese broccoli, for example. When you pull out the unwanted seedlings, gently press the ground around the one that is left so that the pulling motion does not disturb it as well.

THINNING SEEDLINGS *IN SITU*

When thinning a row of seedlings that have been sown *in situ*, remove the unwanted plants, leaving the recommended gap between each retained plant. Water the seedlings before and after thinning.

When the row is complete, gently water along its length so that soil is washed back around the roots of the remaining plants that may have been disturbed. Dispose of the unwanted seedlings on the compost heap.

Avoid thinning during hot or windy weather. The plants left in the ground may have been disturbed during the thinning process and their roots will dry out before they have a chance to re-establish themselves. A slightly damp, overcast day is ideal.

In hot, dry weather, you can snip off the unwanted seedlings with a pair of scissors so that you do not disturb the roots of the neighbouring plants.

TRANSPLANTING

Plants for transplanting can either be grown from seed sown in pots or trays, or from seed sown directly in the open ground. Seedlings that have been grown in containers should be pricked out first into individual pots, or widely spaced in trays, so that each plant has room to develop. Harden them off if they have been grown under glass before transplanting them into the ground.

Damp, overcast weather conditions are ideal for transplanting seedlings because the plants will not dry out quickly in a muggy atmosphere. Again, as with thinning, it is essential to water the plants first before transplanting them. This will give them sufficient moisture to keep them going until they have re-established their root systems.

PLANT DISTANCES

Thinning
Lettuce: 23cm/9in
Spinach: 15cm/6in
Swiss chard: 30cm/12in

Transplanting
Brussels sprouts: 50–75cm/ 20–30in
Cabbages: 30–50cm/12–20in
Calabrese: 15–23cm/6–9in
Cauliflowers: 50–75cm/20–30in
Kale: 60cm/24in
Sprouting broccoli: 60cm/24in

Dig up just a few plants at a time – there is no point in leaving plants lying around on the ground where they can dry out. Discard any that are undernourished or weak, and never use any that are diseased. Using a line to make sure that the row is straight and a measuring stick in order to get the planting distances correct, plant at the same depth as in the seed bed to prevent rot. Gently firm in around each plant and water in.

USING A DIBBER

Cabbages (shown here), onions and leeks are planted out using a dibber. This makes a hole in the ground into which the plant is slipped before the earth is firmed in around it.

Weeding

Many people are put off gardening simply because they do not like the idea of weeding. However, there are two points that they probably never consider. The first is that in a well-maintained garden there is far less weeding to do than they might think, and, second, weeding can be a relaxing, even therapeutic, task.

KEEP IT CLEAN

Weeds take nutrients and moisture from the soil, depriving the vegetables of their share. They can grow tall, smothering or drawing up the vegetables so that they do not grow properly. Many weeds harbour diseases, particularly rusts, and pass these on to your crops. So keep your kitchen garden clear of weeds if you want to produce the best crops.

GOOD PREPARATION

One way to reduce the amount of weeding is to prepare the ground thoroughly, removing all weeds, particularly roots of perennial weeds, by hand or with weedkillers. You will then have to deal only with new weed seedlings, which are not a problem as long as they are hoed off soon after they have appeared. If you remove them before they can run to seed, gradually the number of seeds left in the soil will be reduced.

KEEPING ON TOP

As long as you keep on top of weeds they are not a problem, but when you let things slip it can become a chore. Hoeing off weed seedlings as they appear will take only a few minutes. Allow them to become fully grown and it will take hours to remove them.

HOEING

The method of hoeing is often a matter of personal preference. If you have a draw or swan-neck hoe, you scrape the weeds off by drawing the hoe towards you. If you have a plate or Dutch hoe, push it forwards to slice off the weeds. If you have a three-pronged cultivator, pull it through the top layer of soil to disturb the roots of the weeds. In dry weather a hoe of either kind is best because if you open the soil too much water will evaporate. In wetter weather, however, the cultivator can be useful because it opens the soil and allows water to drain through.

CLOSE WORK

Weeds do not always conveniently grow between the rows; they also

ABOVE Hoeing is the traditional way of keeping a vegetable garden free of weeds. Pull a draw hoe or swan-neck hoe towards you in a series of chopping movements.

grow in them where it is not as easy to hoe. With well-spaced crops, such as cabbages, it is possible to hoe around them, and sometimes there is space to use an onion hoe, a small hoe with a short handle, which is held in one hand. When you are working close to vegetables be careful not to disturb them. If a vegetable is disturbed, firm down the soil and water in afterwards. Also be careful not to damage the stem or root of the plant as this can allow in diseases.

ABOVE A cultivator is a three-pronged tool that is drawn between the rows of vegetables. This loosens the earth and with it any seedlings that have just germinated. As their roots are loose, they die.

ABOVE It is not always possible to hoe if the weeds are too well advanced, or if the vegetables are close together and might be damaged. Weeding with a hand fork is then the best alternative.

Pests and diseases

One of the best ways of reducing pest damage in the garden is to grow a wide range of crops. A mixed garden will attract a host of wildlife, such as ladybirds, hoverflies and other predators, which will attack any pests that arrive in the garden. Also, if you only grow cabbages and cabbage root fly devastates your crop, you have nothing left. However, if you grow 20 different types of vegetables, you are only going to lose a twentieth of your total crop.

ANIMALS AND BIRDS

Mammals can rarely be killed and are difficult to deter. The only effective action you can take is to build a barricade around your garden. Wire netting should be partially buried in the ground to stop burrowing species, such as rabbits, getting underneath.

BIRDS

The only real recourse against birds such as pigeons is to net everything. Low-level netting can be used as temporary protection when crops are at their most vulnerable.

In addition to eating fruit, buds and leaf vegetables, birds can also cause damage to crops by dust-bathing in seed beds. These can be covered with netting or several pea-sticks can be laid temporarily on the bed.

INSECTS

Some insect pests, such as aphids, attack virtually anything; others, such as cabbage root fly, restrict themselves to one type of crop. Blackfly can be a pest on succulent tips, but small outbreaks of insects can usually be removed by hand before they get out of control.

If the worst comes to the worst, use a chemical control. There are types that are safe to use with vegetables, but read the instructions on the packaging, especially any advice about safety. Use chemicals as a last resort only, and make sure that spray or powder does not drift on to other plants, especially those that may be ready to be harvested.

ABOVE Wire netting can be used to guard crops against rabbits and rodents.

LEFT Birds and butterflies can be kept at bay with fine-meshed nets.

ABOVE Aphids not only distort and weaken plants by sucking the sap from leaves and stems, but they can also introduce diseases.

ABOVE Caterpillars cause a great deal of damage to leaves, especially to members of the cabbage family.

ABOVE Mechanical methods, such as fleece, can be used to cover brassicas to prevent butterflies from laying eggs.

CATERPILLARS

There are three ways of dealing with caterpillars. First, cover the plants with fleece or small-mesh netting so that butterflies and moths cannot lay eggs. Second, check susceptible plants regularly and remove eggs or caterpillars by hand. Third, use chemicals that are suitable for vegetables and follow the instructions scrupulously.

SLUGS AND SNAILS

Among the many traditional ways of ridding the garden of molluscs are using containers of beer sunk into the ground, and going out after dark with a torch (flashlight) to round up and kill as many as you can.

If you must use slug bait always follow the manufacturer's instructions and do not leave either bait or dead slugs around because they may be eaten by wildlife.

RIGHT Biological controls are mainly used in greenhouses, but others are now becoming available for the open garden. The control insects are released, here from a sachet, in order to attack the pests.

DISEASES

Remove diseased or rotting material as soon as you see it. Deter aphids, which often carry disease, and do not use the same ground two years running for the same crop. Wet, ill-drained soil may cause some diseases, so improving the condition of the soil can help to keep disease at bay. Healthy, well-fed and watered plants are less likely to fall prey to disease.

Many modern hybrids are less susceptible to certain diseases than some of the older ones, so choose your varieties with care.

If you do use chemicals, be careful and follow all instructions, especially the safety ones. Store chemicals well out of the reach of young children.

Burning is the only solution for plants suffering from viral diseases, such as mosaic virus on spinach, because there is no known cure.

Use a rotational system of growing crops and do not put diseased plants on the compost heap. Although the compost should get hot enough to kill off any spores, you might end up spreading the disease over the whole garden.

Growing greens organically

As increasing numbers of people become concerned about the levels of artificial insecticides, fungicides and weedkillers used in the commercial production of all vegetables and fruit, the attractions of organically grown produce are becoming self-evident. Greens are ideal crops to grow organically.

ORGANIC GARDENS

There is more to organic gardening than just not using chemicals. Organic gardeners work to improve the quality of the soil to provide plants with the best possible growing conditions. They also aim to develop a natural balance within the garden by attracting wildlife to help combat pests and to pollinate plants, and by growing a wide range of plants. In this way attacks by pests and diseases affect only a small proportion of the entire vegetable plot, and the inclusion of companion plants acts as a positive deterrent to some forms of pest.

Rather than single or double digging the vegetable plot on a regular basis, some organic gardeners prefer the no-dig system. After an initial thorough digging to remove all perennial weed roots and other debris, the soil is gradually built up by the annual addition of mulches of well-rotted compost and manure. Because the ground is not disturbed by digging, the soil is not unnecessarily aerated and the natural layers of soil that develop over time are not destroyed.

ABOVE A good mixed garden, with plenty of varieties of flowers and vegetables, is less likely to have problems than one restricted to a monoculture. It will attract insects, which in turn attack pests.

GREEN MANURE

In addition to regular applications of well-rotted compost or manure, organic gardeners often sow green manures in ground that has become vacant as a crop is cleared after harvesting. These plants, which include alfalfa, some types of beans and peas and *Phacelia tanacetifolia*, are dug into the ground before they have set seed and are valuable for fixing nitrogen in the soil.

BIOLOGICAL CONTROLS

Whenever predators appear, organic gardeners choose not to spray their crops with insecticides and other chemicals. Biological controls, which are increasingly widely available, are the ideal way of controlling many common pests.

Introduce them as soon as the first signs of attack are noticed, and do not use any insecticides at all once a biological control has been introduced. Be patient and accept that there will be some damage before the biological agent takes effect. When you use biological controls there will always be some pests – they are essential for the predator to continue to breed – but the population will be reduced.

cultivating
greens

Green vegetables are very easy to grow. Sowing and thinning distances and planting times do vary from plant to plant, of course, but these are summarized for each plant to make growing them even easier. Follow the guidelines outlined here and you will have vegetables all year round. Most gardeners have their favourite varieties, chosen because of their taste, appearance or ease of growing, but it is a good idea to try at least a few new varieties each season. This makes gardening more fun as well as giving you an opportunity to discover even better and more interesting green vegetables.

Growing cabbages

Cabbages do best in an open, sunny site in a soil that is fertile but reasonably free draining. They do not like a soil that is too acid, and acid soil may need liming to bring it to a pH of 6.5–7. This should be done immediately after digging and before planting. Most gardeners sow cabbages in nursery beds and transplant them; others prefer to sow them in trays under glass; still others buy them as young plants from nurseries. The methods are basically the same in each case; it is just the timing that varies.

Thinly sow seed in shallow drills about 1cm/½in deep. Thin seedlings if necessary to prevent them from becoming drawn. After about five weeks, when they have four or five leaves, transplant them to their final position. Final spacing depends on the type and size (see Cultivation). Plant using a dibber or trowel and firm the soil in well around the roots. Water well and keep watered until they have become established.

Spring cabbages can be sown *in situ* and initially thinned to 10cm/4in. In spring thin again to 30–38cm/12–15in.

Hoe regularly and keep free of weeds. Draw up some soil around the stems of overwintering varieties. Remove any dead leaves.

HARVESTING

Cut the hearting cabbages when they have become firm. Use a knife to cut through the stem, just below the firm head but inside any loose leaves. Savoy cabbages taste better if they are harvested after they have experienced at least one frost. The leaves of spring cabbages are cut as required, a few being left to heart up if required.

STORAGE

Most cabbages are winter hardy and can be left where they are until required. Those with solid heads can be cut and stored in a cool place, where they will keep for a couple of months. Some varieties of

ABOVE A block of mature cabbages in very good condition.

red cabbages may not be as hardy and can be harvested in early winter and stored.

PESTS AND DISEASES

Cabbage root fly are a nuisance, but they can be deterred by placing a collar of roofing felt or a similar material around the plant's stem. This prevents the adults from laying their eggs near the plant. Caterpillars are another problem. Cover the plants with netting or fleece to stop butterflies laying their

STARTING CABBAGES

Cabbage plants can be started in a cold frame before moving to their final growing position.

PROTECTING YOUNG CABBAGES

Young cabbages need protecting from birds. Wire guards are light, and also easy to store if they are made in sections.

GROWTH BOOSTERS

Spring cabbages often benefit from a light dressing of a nitrogenous fertilizer to stimulate the growth of fresh young leaves.

eggs. Caterpillars can be removed by hand, but if you decide to spray, follow the manufacturer's instructions. Flea beetles make small holes in young leaves and should be prevented by dusting with the appropriate chemical. Slugs and snails should be controlled. The most serious disease is club root, which causes the roots to swell up. Any affected plants should be burned or destroyed. Liming helps to deter club root, as does crop rotation, so that cabbages grow in a different bed each year.

BELOW Green manure can be grown as a separate crop or between existing crops. When clover is grown among cabbages it not only fixes nitrogen in the soil but also helps to keep down weeds.

CULTIVATION

Spring cabbage
Sowing time: late summer
Sowing distance: sow thinly
Sowing depth: 1cm/½in
Distance between sown rows:
  15cm/6in
Planting distance: 30–38cm/
  12–15in
Distance between planted rows:
  50–60cm/20–24in
Harvesting: spring

Summer cabbage
Sowing time: early to mid-spring
Sowing distance: sow thinly
Sowing depth: 1cm/½in
Distance between sown rows:
  15cm/6in
Planting distance: 35cm/14in
Distance between planted rows:
  60cm/24in
Harvesting: midsummer onwards

Autumn cabbage
Sowing time: late spring
Sowing distance: sow thinly
Sowing depth: 1cm/½in
Distance between sown rows:
  15cm/6in
Planting distance: 50cm/20in
Distance between planted rows:
  60–75cm/24–30in
Harvesting: autumn

Winter cabbage
Sowing time: late spring
Sowing distance: sow thinly
Sowing depth: 1cm/½in
Distance between sown rows:
  15cm/6in
Planting distance: 50cm/20in
Distance between planted rows:
  60–75cm/24–30in
Harvesting: winter

Growing Brussels sprouts

Brussels sprouts require an open position, but it should be protected from strong winds. The ground should be manured in autumn and limed if necessary to bring the acidity to within pH 6.5–7. The seed can be sown in the open ground or started in trays under cover. For a late-summer picking the seed should be sown in late winter or early spring; soil and weather conditions would generally mean that these seeds should be sown inside. For the more usual autumn-onwards harvest sow in the open in early to mid-spring. Sow the earliest varieties first and the latest a few weeks later to make sure that they crop successionally. Sow thinly in shallow drills (see Cultivation).

Plant out in the final position about five weeks after sowing, when the plants are about 13cm/5in tall. Plant the taller varieties at 75cm/30in intervals and the dwarfer forms at 50cm/20in intervals, with 75cm/30in between rows. Use a dibber or a trowel and firm the soil lightly around the plant. Water well.

Keep the plants well watered until they are established. Because there is such a large amount of space between plants they can be intercropped with a fast-growing crop, such as lettuces. Keep the weeds down. If the site is exposed, stake the plants against the wind. Drawing soil up around the stems also helps. Remove the bottom leaves as they turn yellow.

CULTIVATION

Sowing time: early to mid-spring
Sowing distance: sow thinly
Sowing depth: 1cm/½in
Distance between sown rows:
   15cm/6in
Planting-out: when 13cm/5in high
Planting distance: 50–75cm/
   20–30in
Distance between planted rows:
   75cm/30in
Harvesting: mid-autumn to spring

HARVESTING
Pick the Brussels sprouts when they are large enough to use but still tight. Start at the bottom of the plant,

BELOW These Brussels sprouts have been decoratively planted with red cabbages.

picking a few off each plant and snapping off each one with a downward twist. Move up the stems as the sprouts fill out. When all the sprouts are removed, pick the loose heads or tops and cook them as greens. Most gardeners prefer not to start harvesting until after the first frosts because this improves the flavour. As you harvest, remove any sprouts that have not formed tight balls but are just a loose collection of leaves and put them on the compost heap.

STORAGE

Brussels sprouts are hardy and can be left on the stems until they are required. They cannot be stored after picking for any length of time unless they are frozen. Freeze early maturing varieties before the weather damages the outer leaves. Choose only good quality, uniform sprouts for freezing.

PESTS AND DISEASES

Brussels sprouts are prone to the same problems as cabbages. The worst problem is club root. Aphids

will also take shelter in the tightly packed sprouts. Constant vigilance will help you detect them.

ABOVE Purple-leaved Brussels sprouts make a striking combination with *Dahlia* 'Bishop of Llandaff' through the fence.

TRANSPLANTING SEEDLINGS GROWN IN A SEEDBED

1 If the plants are well spaced, lift each individually with a trowel. If they are too close for this, loosen the soil with a fork and pull them up carefully.

2 Plant with a trowel and firm the soil well. Insert the blade of the trowel about 5cm/2in away from the plant and press it firmly towards the roots.

3 All brassicas need to be planted firmly. Test this by tugging a leaf after planting. Always water in thoroughly after transplanting.

Growing sprouting broccoli

An open position is required, preferably one not buffeted by strong winds. The ground should be reasonably rich, manured in autumn and limed if necessary to bring the acidity to a pH of 6.5–7. The seed can be sown in spring in the open ground or started in modules or trays under cover. Sow thinly in shallow drills 1cm/½in deep. If necessary, thin to 5cm/2in apart. Transplant the young broccoli when they are about 13cm/5in high. Water the row of plants the day before transplanting. Plant out the young broccoli at 60cm/24in intervals with the same distance between rows, using a dibber or trowel. Firm them in well with your heel and water.

Keep watered until they are established. Remove any weeds as soon as you notice them. In windy areas it may be necessary to stake the plants to prevent wind-rock. Earthing (hilling) up the stems will also help.

HARVESTING

Depending on the cultivar you have selected, harvesting starts in late winter to mid-spring. Snap or cut off the shoots as they begin to bud up but before they come into flower. Shoots should be about 15cm/6in long. Pick the shoots from all parts of the plant. Do not allow any to come into flower, or they will quickly run to seed and exhaust the plant.

CULTIVATION

Sowing time: mid-spring
Sowing distance: sow thinly
Sowing depth: 1cm/½in
Distance between sown rows: 15cm/6in
Planting-out time: when 13cm/5in high
Planting distance: 60cm/24in
Distance between planted rows: 60–75cm/24–30in
Harvesting: late winter to mid-spring

STORAGE

Broccoli is perfectly hardy and should be left on the plant until required. It will not keep for more than a few days after picking, although it can be stood in a jug of water to keep it fresh or placed in a cool place such as a refrigerator. It can be stored for longer periods by freezing, a good way of coping with excess heads, which should always be picked and not left on the plant to flower.

PESTS AND DISEASES

Broccoli is susceptible to the same problems as cabbages. Like other brassicas, broccoli should not be grown in the same ground two years running to minimize the chances of club root taking hold. As they are in the ground over winter, they make inviting food for hungry birds, so make certain they are well protected with netting.

LEFT This purple sprouting broccoli is now ready for cutting.

Growing calabrese broccoli

Sow calabrese broccoli (Italian sprouting broccoli) and romanesco (Roman broccoli) in an open site in a fertile soil that has either been manured for a previous crop or manured during autumn digging. It is important to sow where they are to mature, because they do not transplant well. Station sow in shallow drills about 1cm/½in deep at 30cm/12in intervals. Sow three seeds at each station. Rows should be 30cm/12in apart. Seeds can be sown closer together but this results in smaller heads. After germination, remove surplus seedlings so that only one, the strongest, remains at each station to grow on.

Keep well watered, especially in dry spells, so that the plants' growth is not checked. Keep them free of weeds.

HARVESTING

Depending on the variety you grow, calabrese broccoli is ready for harvesting from summer until well into autumn, and usually takes 10–12 weeks after sowing to be ready to pick. Romanesco is ready from late autumn to early winter or even later if the plants are protected with cloches.

Calabrese broccoli first produces a single head, which should be cut while the buds are still tightly closed. Some varieties will subsequently produce side shoots, although these have smaller heads, like sprouting broccoli. Romanesco produces only a single head, and when this is harvested the entire plant can be disposed of in the compost bin.

STORAGE

Neither calabrese nor romanesco keeps for more than a few days in a cool place, and both are best eaten straight from the plant. They can be preserved for longer by freezing. Fresh heads can be kept for a few days in the refrigerator by standing them in water.

CULTIVATION

Calabrese broccoli (Italian sprouting broccoli)
Sowing time: successional sowings from mid- to early summer
Sowing distance: station sow at 30cm/12in
Sowing depth: 1cm/½in
Distance between sown rows: 30cm/12in
Harvesting: late summer to autumn

Romanesco (Roman broccoli)
Sowing time: early summer
Sowing distance: station sow at 30cm/12in
Sowing depth: 1cm/½in
Distance between sown rows: 30cm/12in
Harvesting: late autumn to early winter (later if protected)

PESTS AND DISEASES

Both vegetables are susceptible to the same problems as cabbages, especially club root. Adopt a policy of regular crop rotation to avoid using the same soil for two consecutive years.

STATION SOWING

Calabrese broccoli needs to be sown where it is to grow. Station sow the seed at intervals of 30cm/12in.

HARVESTING

Use a sharp knife to cut cleanly under the closed head. Take some of the stem as this can be eaten as well.

Growing kale

Kale needs an open situation in which to grow. Although it prefers a fertile soil, it will grow in poorer soils than most other members of the brassica family. If possible, however, incorporate well-rotted manure when digging in autumn. Thinly sow the seed in late spring in the open ground in drills that are about 1cm/½in deep and 20cm/8in apart. Thin if necessary so that the young plants are about 5cm/2in apart. Transplant to their final positions when they are about 13cm/5in high. The final planting distances vary depending on the variety – for smaller varieties 30–45cm/12–18in will do, but the largest may need to be 60–75cm/24–30in apart. Allow 60cm/24in between the rows.

Kale needs to be kept steadily growing because it is slow to recover from any checks. It is, therefore, necessary to water thoroughly during dry spells, especially when the plants are young. Weed regularly and remove any yellowing leaves.

HARVESTING

With early varieties, harvesting can begin in autumn and continue through winter and into spring. Some forms of kale are ready to harvest about seven weeks after the seed is sown.

Pick the young leaves but do not strip plants, as they will take time to recover. It is better to remove just a few leaves from each plant. In spring pick the emerging shoots before they come into flower. Leaves and shoots are picked simply by snapping them off.

CULTIVATION

Sowing time: late spring
Sowing distance: sow thinly
Sowing depth: 1cm/½in
Distance between sown rows: 20cm/8in
Planting-out time: when 13cm/5in high
Planting distance: 30–75cm/12–30in
Distance between planted rows: 60cm/24in
Harvesting: autumn to mid-spring

STORAGE

Kale is extremely hardy, and the leaves can be left on the plants until required. It cannot be stored for long, although it can be frozen for use between spring and the first of the summer vegetables. Picked leaves will keep fresh briefly in the refrigerator, in a jug of water.

WATERING

It is important that kale plants are kept growing, so make sure that you do not let the soil dry out. Water well, as required.

HARVESTING

Narrow-leaved black kale is being harvested here by removing the younger, more succulent leaves.

PESTS AND DISEASES

Kale is generally the most trouble-free of all the brassicas, but it is still prone to the same problems as cabbages. Caterpillars can be a particular problem with autumn-picked varieties, especially because they hide within the curly leaves. Treatment with a spray or powder may help if it gets into the creases. Alternatively, spray with the bacterium *Bacillus thuringiensis*, which is fatal to the caterpillars of the cabbage white butterfly but is completely harmless to humans.

ABOVE This informal vegetable garden includes a block of young curly kale plants. Kale is a decorative addition to any garden.

RIGHT When harvesting, it is better to pick just a few leaves from each plant. They are picked by simply snapping them off. Soaking them in salted water before you cook them is a good way to remove caterpillars.

Growing cauliflower

Cauliflowers can be difficult to grow, but, with care and attention, all gardeners should be able to produce good-quality crops. The main factor is to make sure that the plants' growth is not checked, because this causes irregular and undersized curds. An irregular water supply can be one cause. Late transplanting may be another. The one aspect that is difficult for the gardener to control is high summer temperatures, which are not conducive to growing good cauliflowers, since they prefer cool conditions. In hot areas you may have to abandon the idea of summer cauliflowers and concentrate on winter varieties.

Cauliflowers should be planted in an open, sunny position. To grow cauliflowers well it is essential that you have a fertile soil, preferably manured during digging in autumn. The manure is important, because the soil should be moisture-retentive so that the plants are not checked during dry periods. The soil must not be too acid; if possible adjust the pH level to 6.5–7 by liming in autumn.

The seeds can be sown in the open ground or in modules or trays. They should be sown thinly in shallow drills about 1cm/½in deep and 20cm/8in apart. For the timing for the various seasons, check the Cultivation box. If necessary, thin the seedlings to about 5cm/2in apart. Transplant them when they have five leaves, which should be about six weeks after sowing. Water the rows of seedlings on the day and then

Cauliflowers are often raised in modules so that the seedlings receive less of a shock when they are transplanted. Many modules are designed so that you can remove the plant by gently squeezing the base while carefully supporting the plant at the top.

transplant them using a dibber or trowel. Firm down the soil around the plant with your heel. The planting distances vary from 50cm/20in to 75cm/30in, depending on the variety. Keep cauliflowers well watered, especially in warm, dry spells. Once the curds begin to form, snap the larger outside leaves down over them to protect them. This will prevent discoloration.

HARVESTING

The curds are ready when they form an even dome shape. Summer and autumn varieties mature in about 16 weeks from sowing and winter ones in about 40 weeks.

LEFT These freshly harvested baby cauliflowers are ready for eating.

Mini varieties are ready in about 15 weeks. When they are ready, cut through the stem with a sharp knife just below the head, leaving one or two leaves around the curd to protect it on its way to the kitchen. If you are storing them for a while, cut them so that they have a short length of stem from which you can hang them.

STORAGE

In general, it is best to leave the cauliflowers on the plants until they are required, but they can be cut and kept in a cool place for some time if necessary. They store best if they are hung upside down. If the leaves are occasionally sprayed with water, they will keep for several weeks in cool conditions. They can also be frozen.

PESTS AND DISEASES

Cauliflowers are susceptible to the same problems as cabbages. To avoid the possibility of club root disease do not grow cauliflowers in the same ground for two years running.

CULTIVATION

Early summer
Sowing time: midwinter
Sowing position: under glass
Planting-out time: spring, when 13cm/5in high
Planting distance: 50cm/20in
Distance between planted rows: 60cm/24in
Harvesting: early to midsummer

Summer
Sowing time: mid-spring
Sowing distance: sow thinly
Sowing depth: 1cm/½in
Distance between sown rows: 20cm/8in
Planting-out time: early summer, when 13cm/5in high
Planting distance: 60cm/24in
Distance between planted rows: 60–75cm/24–30in
Harvesting: late summer

Autumn
Sowing time: late spring
Sowing distance: sow thinly
Sowing depth: 1cm/½in
Distance between sown rows: 20cm/8in
Planting-out time: early summer, when 13cm/5in high
Planting distance: 60cm/24in
Distance between planted rows: 60–75cm/24–30in
Harvesting: autumn

Winter
Sowing time: late spring
Sowing distance: sow thinly
Sowing depth: 1cm/½in
Distance between sown rows: 20cm/8in
Planting-out time: summer, when 13cm/5in high
Planting distance: 70–75cm/28–30in
Distance between planted rows: 60–75cm/24–30in
Harvesting: late winter to early spring

Mini-cauliflowers
Sowing time: spring
Sowing distance: station sow 15cm/6in
Sowing depth: 1cm/½in
Distance between sown rows: 45cm/18in
Harvesting: late summer to autumn

PLANTING

Cauliflowers must be firmed in well when they are planted. Plants in loose soil run to seed quickly.

PREVENTING SUN SCORCH

Protect the developing curds from discoloration by the sun by covering them with the inner leaves.

HARVESTING

Harvest the cauliflower by cutting the stem with a sharp knife just below the first ring of leaves.

Growing spinach

Grow spinach in an open, sunny position but preferably one that does not get too hot. The soil should be fertile and contain as much organic material as possible so that it is moisture-retentive. Permanently wet soils should be avoided, however. Dig in manure or compost in autumn.

Thinly sow the seed in early spring, with successional sowings at two-week intervals through to late spring. It is better to sow several short or part-rows at intervals than one long one if there is the possibility that most of the plants will run to seed before they are harvested. Sow in shallow drills, about 1cm/½in deep, and 30cm/12in apart. As soon as the seedlings are big enough to handle, thin them out to 15cm/6in apart. Keep well watered and weeded.

A crop for overwintering can be sown in late summer or early autumn. This will benefit from being covered with cloches from autumn onwards. The cloches will not only protect the plants, but will keep the leaves tender.

New Zealand spinach can be sown under glass and transplanted or sown direct in shallow drills after the last frosts. Pinch out the tips to make plants bush out. Red orach can be sown in drills or by scattering the seeds.

HARVESTING

Start harvesting as soon as the leaves are big enough, which is usually 8–12 weeks after sowing. Don't strip the plant, but just take a few leaves to start with and continue until the plants are mature. Break or cut the stems, but avoid pulling because this may loosen the plant and precipitate bolting. Continue harvesting until the plants start to run to seed – when the central stem starts to elongate. When harvesting winter spinach, do not overpick.

STORAGE

Spinach should be picked and used as fresh as possible because it does not keep well. The leaves can, however, be frozen. If necessary, they can be stored in a jug of water in the refrigerator for a day or so.

LEFT This row of succulent-looking spinach is now ready for harvesting.

CULTIVATION

Summer

Sowing time: successional sowings from early to late spring
Sowing distance: sow thinly
Sowing depth: 1cm/½in
Thinning distance: 15cm/6in
Distance between sown rows: 30cm/12in
Harvesting: early to late summer

Winter

Sowing time: late summer to early autumn
Sowing distance: sow thinly
Sowing depth: 1cm/½in
Thinning distance: 15cm/6in
Distance between sown rows: 30cm/12in
Harvesting: winter and spring

Harvesting

Spinach is a very easy crop to harvest. When you require some, simply cut away the young leaves with a pair of sharp scissors.

PESTS AND DISEASES

Spinach should be grown so fast that there can be few problems (apart from bolting) and, in any case, there is little time for the gardener to satisfactorily correct any problems that do occur. The best solution in this case is to discard the affected plants and start again.

To avoid slug damage, clear the ground of slugs before sowing and at regular intervals thereafter. The diseases most likely to affect spinach are downy mildew (choose resistant varieties) and spinach blight. Destroy the affected plants.

Although not a disease, bolting can be a problem. Bolting is the tendency of a plant to rapidly flower and go to seed. This can be minimized by having a moisture-retentive soil and watering regularly. Some varieties are more bolt-resistant than others, so check before buying the seed.

ABOVE When harvesting, simply cut away the young leaves with a pair of scissors.

RIGHT A healthy crop of spinach is one element in this beautifully maintained walled potager.

Growing Swiss chard

Swiss chard and perpetual spinach need an open site and a fertile soil. Manure the soil while digging it in the autumn. Station sow the chard in spring in shallow drills 1cm/½in deep and 38cm/15in apart. The stations should be 45cm/18in apart for larger plants, although for smaller plants they can be closer together. For perpetual spinach the intervals should be 30cm/12in. Germination will be within a few days. Thin out unwanted seedlings at each station. A sowing can be made in late summer to provide a crop that goes on until the following summer, which, together with the spring sowing, will provide leaves all year round. Water the plants and keep them weed free.

Both plants can be sown in trays or modules and planted out when they have reached an adequate size, at the same intervals as above. In very cold areas it may be necessary to give the plants the protection of cloches or horticultural fleece, but they are generally hardy enough to need no protection.

HARVESTING

Both forms, Swiss chard and perpetual spinach, are perpetual in that once they have matured (usually 8–12 weeks after sowing) leaves can be cut from them as you wish, right through from summer until the following spring when they are likely to start running to seed. (Swiss chard in seed is a very decorative vegetable indeed, so do not be in too much of a hurry to get rid of it unless you desperately need the space.) Snap or cut off the leaves at the base of the plant. Take the leaves as soon as they are big enough and continue to harvest them so that the outer leaves do not get too large and coarse.

STORAGE

Neither plant stores well and leaves should be cooked soon after picking. They will keep for a day or so standing in water in a refrigerator, or they can be frozen.

PESTS AND DISEASES

On the whole, both plants are pest and disease free. However, it is difficult to grow perfect Swiss chard (the leaves always seem to have holes in them), but while this may be a problem on the show bench, once cut up in the kitchen, no one will notice. Slugs, caterpillars, flea beetles, earwigs and birds may all be to blame, but apart from getting rid of the slugs there is no need for action. If planted too close together vegetables may suffer from downy mildew, especially in a damp season.

LEFT This row of mixed colour Swiss chard is ready for harvesting.

WINTER PROTECTION

In cold areas Swiss chard may need some form of winter protection. Any form of cloche or portable cold frame will be suitable.

MULCHING

Mulching with a layer of grass cuttings helps to conserve the moisture in the soil. Water before mulching and do not use too thick a layer as this may heat up and burn the plant – 7.5cm/3in is sufficient.

HARVESTING

Swiss chard is harvested by cutting the stalks at the base with a sharp knife. Like perpetual spinach, it can be harvested from summer until the following spring.

ABOVE A perfect specimen of Swiss chard, clearly showing the white ribs, which can be cooked separately from the leaves.

Growing lettuce

Lettuces need an open, sunny position, although partial shade during the heat of the day can be an advantage in hot areas or in hot summers. The soil must be fertile and, preferably, moisture-retentive, and this is best achieved by incorporating plenty of manure in autumn. Lettuces can be sown straight in the ground or grown in trays and transplanted.

Sow a short row of lettuces and then, instead of throwing away the thinnings, transplant them to make up the rest of the row. The transplants will take a few days to settle down and will produce a slightly later crop than the sown plants. If the whole row is sown at once, the lettuces will mature at the same time, which will probably mean that many are wasted.

Start early sowings in trays or modules under glass in late winter or early spring. Plant these out under cloches or in cold frames to get an early crop. Seed can be sown directly in the soil from early spring onwards. Sow in shallow drills 1cm/½in deep, each row about 30cm/12in apart. Thin the lettuces to 15–30cm/6–12in apart, depending on the size of the variety. Transplanted lettuces should be planted at the same distances. Keep the soil moist and do not allow growth to be checked or they will rapidly run to seed. Sowings after midsummer will provide lettuces for autumn and early winter, but cover them with cloches when necessary from around mid-autumn.

HARVESTING

Lettuces can be harvested whole or leaves can be taken from the plants as required. The loose-leaved varieties are usually picked leaf by leaf, and cabbage-type varieties can be picked in the same way if you wish. Hearted varieties are usually ready for harvesting as soon as they feel plump and firm. Do not leave them too long in the ground after maturing or they may bolt. Pull the whole lettuce from the ground or cut below the bottom leaves if you want the plant to resprout. Loose-leaved varieties mature earlier, and leaves can be picked as soon as they are large enough, usually from about seven weeks after sowing.

STORAGE

Whole lettuces can be kept in a refrigerator for a short time but are best used straight from the garden.

PESTS AND DISEASES

Slugs and greenfly (aphids) are two of the worst problems. Other pests include root aphids and cutworms.

The main disease is downy mildew, and in wet seasons lettuces also tend to suffer from a few other fungal diseases. Make sure that lettuces are not planted too close together so that air can circulate around the plants. If pests or diseases do get out of control, get rid of the plants and start again.

CULTIVATION

Sowing time: late winter (under glass) to early spring onwards
Sowing distance: sow thinly
Sowing depth: 1cm/½in
Distance between sown rows: 30cm/12in
Thinning distance: 15–30cm/ 6–12in
Harvesting: early summer onwards

INTERCROPPING

Plant lettuces between slower growing plants. They will be harvested before the cabbages overshadow them.

HARVESTING

Harvest lettuces when the hearts feel firm when you gently squeeze them. Pull the whole lettuce or cut below the leaves.

Growing salad leaves

All these salad leaves are plants for a cool climate and will rapidly run to seed in hotter areas. Because of this and because other salad materials are scarce at that time, they are mainly grown for autumn and winter use. In cooler areas they can be sown in spring for summer use. Although they are hardy, they need to be protected by cloches to be at their best.

Both rocket (arugula) and lamb's lettuce (mâche) are sown in late summer; rocket can also be sown in early autumn. Sow in drills 1cm/½in deep and 30cm/12in apart. Thin the seedlings to 15cm/6in apart for rocket and to 10cm/4in for lamb's lettuce. Keep lettuces watered in dry weather. Cover with cloches in late autumn or early winter.

HARVESTING AND STORAGE

Either pick individual leaves or cut them all as soon as they are large enough. They will sprout again.

Both plants should be picked as required because they will not keep for more than a few hours.

PESTS AND DISEASES

Both plants should be free of both pests and diseases, although rocket may be attacked by flea beetle. If the tell-tale small holes appear on the leaves, dust with derris. Apart from flea beetle, there may also be a problem with the plants bolting,

ABOVE Lamb's lettuce does not store well, and needs eating immediately.

that is, rapidly flowering and turning to seed. This can be delayed by ensuring that the plants are well watered so that they continue to grow rather than using their remaining strength to flower.

CULTIVATION

Rocket (arugula)
Sowing time: late summer to early
  autumn
Sowing distance: sow thinly
Sowing depth: 1cm/½in
Distance between sown rows:
  30cm/12in
Thinning distance: 15cm/6in
Harvesting: late autumn onwards

Lamb's lettuce (mâche)
Sowing time: late summer
Sowing distance: sow thinly
Sowing depth: 1cm/½in
Distance between sown rows:
  30cm/12in
Thinning distance: 10cm/4in
Harvesting: winter

SOWING LAMB'S LETTUCE

Try sowing lamb's lettuce as a cold month crop. They don't need cloche protection except in particularly cold areas, but the cover will ensure a better supply of more succulent leaves.

PROTECTING CROPS

Put the cloches in position before the cold weather checks growth. With a little protection like this the plants will crop more freely. It will also protect the plants from splashing mud.

Index